Poems, Short Stories, Thoughts, & Life Events

All from a Crazy Person

Normally this is where people get thanked and all that shit. There is one here. The only thing I have to thank is the voices in my crazy mind that gives you these things to read. If you enjoy or not, this started as a blog in 2012 until now, if anything it may bring something's to light.

Thank you for the photos Lori Vuckovich. All pictures belong to her.

Name	Page Number

New Life Chapter

Today starts a new day in my life where things must change. I am not sure if I have wronged people or I have been just mistaken things. Most people would be upset and heart broken in the situation that I am in, but I am trying to stay positive and move forward in the ways that I think and act. My life is not defined by someone else it is defined by me. I have spent too much time and effort being someone I am not, so I will no longer be who everyone else wants me to be. If you don't like me, I no longer am going to give a shit. Is that simple enough?

I have spent years trying to figure out people, mainly women in my life. Never before have I been given the opportunity to think for myself and do what I believe is right for me. I am no longer taking advice or having someone take care of me. It's time for me to be single and proud to be alone, I don't know myself, and that blows. I can sit in the same spot for hours doing nothing and that is all I do. There is more to life than just that.

I am not putting my life on hold or saying no to anyone. I just need time to figure out what went wrong in my life over the last twenty years and move on from there. I have not shut down, I do look forward to tomorrow, and welcome the learning experiences that I must live with from the past and figure everything out.

Tear Staining

The night is late and the moon is high with the sky and the stillness of the chilled air brings thoughts that should be lost in time brought out to the fore front. There they lay on the table but the mind has checked out and is giving zero help. The heart only beats and just keeps the body alive without the emotion.

Everyone has the opinion of what to do and what to say to help. There is nothing that anyone can do that will change what is on the table. The old wooden table has stood the test of time just sitting there. It has seen a lot and if it could talk it would say things that would blow the mind out of its head, but it just sits there.

The chill air surrounds the body and makes skin turn to goose bumps. It brings energy of calmness. The air doesn't say anything new and it doesn't change what is already known. The chill freezes the slow moving tears that have slide over the cheeks on the face. The inhale of the chilled air and energy fills the lungs.

Energy flows through the veins and circulates all through the body. It moves swiftly and makes the hands grab the chair. The body tenses up with pain with the eyes closed with the frozen tears hitting the palms of the hands that have moved to the face.

Elbows on the table and the back crouched over with the face in the hands. Tears have covered the skin and runs down the arms to the wooden table. The stain on the table turns darker from the dampness. Then without reason everything stops and there is no more crying. The brain wonders why the sadness? There hasn't been a thought to make these things happen.

Anger pushes the energy that flows through the veins. The hands grab the end of the table and the arms push the body away sliding the also wooden, matching table back from the former position. The lungs breathe deep and suck in air through the mouth as the nose is stuffed and is no longer cooperating. The legs stand the body up moving to the window and waits while the eyes glair out into nothingness.

The brain activates and wonders about what has happened. It knows that something has happened and cannot rationalize the reasoning behind it. How was the brain shut down? How did the emptiness enter the body and take control? The brain worries but the subconscious makes the legs move and carry the body somewhere else. In this place the subconscious has planned something for the brain to do so it does not worry of the event that has happened until the next time it happens...

Edge of the Bed

Night has been sucked out of the air and there is nothing left in the darkness. What am I to do with the night that won't end? The edge has become the place in which I sit and not move from this place. The phone sings but it's not lullabies that place me to sleep for the night.

It doesn't matter which combination of pills I try I can't sleep without taking too much and meeting the man in black. My Mind has started on overdrive, it's been on idle all day yet there hasn't been a clear thought that has made its way out.

The day brought pain and suffering to an understanding soul, yet again I have let the world down. My heart fell from my sleeve and hit my foot as I kicked it across the room and now I can't find it in this dump. So, I sit and stair into the darkness that turned into a clear line of sight from my eyes adjusting through the tears.

The room's air has grown heavy and the energy hits me in the chest. It feels like it should lift me in the air into the next realm, but I stay. The man in black isn't ready for me. They all enjoy watching me suffer. They all snicker and point while they laugh at the man that fell to his knees as a boy. Lost in a world without the guidance that I should have been given as I was brought up through life, it's not there and not found.

So here it is to the edge of the bed. The seat that isn't a seat, the place I should start to lay down, is now the thought of reflection of the mistakes of life and the day. The past will never be let go and the things that I am to learn from them will never be figured out with the man in black stalking me. Standing over me and waiting. Pushing and prodding me to hurry and speed the process up. The thoughts and the broken glass past is something that I will never get over at this point in my life. One day when I have it figured out he can sit beside me and lay me to rest, until then him and his friends Karma and Fate can continue to laugh at the broken man.

I will pay now for the wrong doings that I have done...

Alone

I never thought that I would have so much trouble being by myself. I constantly am trying to do everything I can to make myself uplifted and happy all the time. Right now, I stare at two tickets to see a Hurt concert and no one to go with. I didn't realize how many bridges I had burned in the last 8 months. Relationship breakups kill friendships sometimes too. I lost a lot of friends with the last few break ups. Some people I am not ashamed of losing but there are some that turned on me in a heartbeat. Ones that I never thought would happen. Though, I know that I have to learn how to live to be by myself in life because I need to. It is one of the things that hold me back in relationships. It's that I don't know myself. It couldn't hurt though to know enough people that would want to go see a concert. I know I messed up my life with people on many things and I can't make up for most of them, but I can apologize and try and move on.

It's time for my life to start moving even if it's alone by me at a concert or a movie. I will live and try to grow stronger, though the beginning blows.

Alone 2 - Growth

I spoke earlier in the week about being alone and needed to learn how to live on my own. The truth is that I am not alone. I sat Tuesday scared to go see Hurt at the Alter Bar in the Strip District in Pittsburgh, Pa that I panicked over. This may seem stupid to most people but my entire life I have always had someone by my side there for me. These people usually live with me and are not hard to convince to do things because they either share the same interest or they care about me and want me to be happy. I realized several things that day that I can do things by myself. I met people at the show who were kind and nice and talked to me like we had known each other for years. For some people this might be normal, but I had never understood these things before.

I have analyzed my life over and repeatedly and I have learned that I am a very selfish and lucky person. I have friends emailing me and commenting on Alone telling me how wonderful of a person I am. I guess when I look at things like being alone, it's not that I am alone it's that I am being selfish and want things to go my way and that's it. My very close friend Brad is here for me every day and yet I consider myself alone. I work with people that are very close friends that will do anything for me.

I wrote Tear Staining about a dog that I feel in love with while in a relationship. I never liked dogs before him, Cecil. He is the greatest dog ever. It wasn't until this Tuesday that I put all the puzzle pieces together that I figured out that it's the unconditional love that I miss. No matter what I did Cecil was there for me. He always wanted to be there for me. I don't know how to make that happen in my life like it was. I will never get to see Cecil again, when I left we said goodbye to each other.

Everything that has leaded me to this point in my life has been by my own doing. I no longer blame anyone for the things that has happened in the past. Clear from when I was a child to the recent mistakes of the last few years to even months. Some people call people like me independent but emotionally people like me are crippled and want what only beautiful Maltese gave me, unconditional love.

Bleach and Blood

Sit away and you see will that a bottle of bleach and a scrubbing pad can't remove this all off of me. The dirt and the hate mixed with vomit makes it all better in the end. When we grab our blades and drop them into the hearts of man by cutting of our sleeves. The mind is dead. The mind has lost its thought.

In the end the red rubs from our skin feeling great and we will remain dirty. The hot shower will be cold when we are done. The bristles will have fallen off and be eaten by the dog. So we pull out our guns and shoot them through our hearts and our sleeves will have holes.

The brain has lost the will to care about anything and can't find its way back to the core. The hair trimmers cut what's in the way for the battery operated drill, but the sleeves of the shirts are nailed to the floor puncturing our hearts and letting them bleed out.

No it all falls from the sink. It falls from the sink. It came, from the sink. Bleach and blood mixed together with the blades and the guns mixed together. The heart still on the floor on my shirt with the dog nibbling at it little by little peppered with bleach and blood.

Bleach and blood mixed with guns and knives, with a shirtless man laid out in the tub. His shirt on the floor with the dog mixing in the bleach, blood, knives and guns. All is found in insanity when found on the floor thinking of imaginary things.

The Truth: No B.S.

I called off sick yesterday and slept until 4pm. To some, people would say that I needed it and that the rest was useful. The thing that really had me concerned though was that no one even texted to see if I was okay. The realization hit me that there wasn't anyone there for me. I have fucked up my life that bad that if something happened there would be no one there. Every time I go to the doctors and try to get fixed for treatment of a pinched nerve, I am asked if I have a Living Will. I don't. I just expect my friends to know what to do. Does anyone know what to do if something happens to me?

Yesterday I hit a low that I never thought I would ever hit. My saving grace was finding someone with a puppy that I hope will love me unconditionally like I will him. If I didn't get that email I don't know where the night would have ended up but things may have been different. I get my pup on Sunday and I can't wait. I can't wait to have something living come into my life and I don't have to worry about fucking things up. I know I am a fuck up and probably deserve to be alone and probably deserve to have a list of people that hate me, I would.

I can't change the past and I can't help the people that I fucked over in this wasted 31 years but all I can do is give this feeling of a last chance, this puppy all that is left in my heart. I don't know if anyone understands this or believes false beliefs but the truth is here in front of you, not everything is the truth but this is. In a fucked up way I am replacing Cecil, the Tear Staining star that I love and miss. This though I hope will give me purpose again, a reason to live again. Before that email...I was nothing and tired and wanted things to be done. I didn't want to die but I wanted to meet the people in the institution because I believed that's where I belonged, and hell maybe I still do.

The front that I put on at work is a very good one and one that maybe even deserve an award, but there isn't many there that are my friends and people that I hang out with at work anymore. I am Straight Edge as much as I can be. I know I take painkillers that goes against that, I don't think I really could make the pinched nerve without it. The fact is that either I have gotten old and am no longer any fun or alcohol isn't that important for me, people chose it over me, just like my father does in fact. That's why I don't drink anymore. I see me falling down the alcoholic path like my father. He drinks a case of beer; I liked Southern Comfort about a half a bottle a night. That world isn't for me, but I am not going to ask anyone to stop drinking. I am not asking anything anymore, the tides have changed, I am no longer important to people as I used to be.

I hope Sunday things change. They have to for my sake.

Pills to make it Better

I have come to the conclusion that I am going to be depressed. I received Maynard yesterday and am nice to have someone around that I know is mine. Though there isn't much that is changed. He is really laid back and likes to sleep a lot. Potty training is going to be a challenge when I have to work the next five days.

It doesn't matter anymore. I went off medicine and I am falling down a path that I can't control. I need help. The help comes in small little pills. As much as I would love to me straight edge fully I can't control my mind. I have to disagree with people here that say medicating yourself is bad when everyone drinks or smokes themselves into oblivion. I want to be a drug free person with the help that I need. August can't come soon enough.

If the pill fixes you to be a better person then I believe that it is okay. I already take Meds for my anxiety, my heart, and a pinched nerve, adding some more shouldn't hurt as long it helps in the long run, because right now the things I do are not helping.

Get Out of Your Mind

I haven't been normal ever. My emotions win and bring me to the creativity that it takes to get you to read this and my book, soon to be books. Things have slowed me down if you have read the blogs. My hand is almost there and ready to type again. People though continue to say that there is something wrong with me, but I say that for the first time possibly ever I am becoming myself. I am becoming more creative and rest inside my head for more thoughts that I can put onto paper or whatever medium I decide. I might not be the same person that I have been in the past but who is. They say the most creative people are the ones with more struggles in their mind. This I believe is the jumping off point to the beginning of the masterpieces that I have planted in my head. They will mess with your head, and you will continue to wonder what, if anything is wrong with me, but I am not the one with problem. The people with the problem are the ones that have a closed mind and can't see the world outside their box. Expand your mind, become one with yourself.

Where Is Your Head? (Another Drug)

I can't find where you have placed the things that pushed on the heart strings. You don't know what you are doing wrong. The push into chemicals is what I have been placed in. Time spent is time hurt. The things that turn me on I hate about me. There is no tomorrow that is clear. Chemicals keep me from falling into the family home. What happened to your head? Why is it that I did nothing wrong but am in trouble. 1...2...3...4...how many pills do I have to take? The collection in my hand looks like lucky charms. The thoughts are no longer mine. Have to get high to function. The heart strings are broken, with heart that was on my sleeve is stomped on. Another session with the therapist brings me feeling like a person but it lasts as long as the drugs. What happened in your head? Would you kill the rabbit and the birds? Insanity takes a form of comfort, I need everything, but instead I end up getting higher. 5...6...7...8...9...10, at the end of the day with no blood spilled, my heart didn't explode, I lay awake every night in the dark and listen to Hurt until the pills get me to the highest and put me down for the day. I know where my head is, but you lost yours on the way, and you stepped away.

I need people to keep reading what I write to stay sane. This is also a drug. I need people to read my book and push me to continue to write. You are now my new drug. Do not disappoint like others.

Look Outside of the Box

Where is the limit? What is a boundary? Why is it OK for you to say that but I can't? Society has destroyed us and most of us don't even know it. We are all truly dead inside. The people sit and stare at a monitor or a giant tricked out screen or use our thumbs to communicate emotionless. We thrive to be in a band so bad that they made a video game so you can feel like you are one. There are games that claim to have us do physical activity as a game but it really does not help anyone.

Why are we all stuck and dead inside. For most people there isn't any creativity inside of you the others are plain and simple, just lazy. No one can hold a person down with goals. I proved that by writing a book. It does not matter if anyone reads it but one person. I accomplished more than a goal, a book, I became alive inside.

We are so quick to judge, which yes I am doing and I have no problem doing that anymore, that we forget that we are the same in our minds as most people that you argue with, or too lazy to do anything about it. Anything could be legal right now if we took after the Occupy group, but we have to be somewhere. You we have been caged. The animals can't harm you if they can't get out, well they did last year. I am proud of the brothers and sisters of the Earth that went and did that, but like I said before, I am also caged.

We blame being brain washed by our parents and for the

most part most people grow up to be them even though you try hard not to be them. If you're brainwashed into thinking that a semi-auto is a good thing to have, that's okay and you don't know better, though I challenge you to look at the statistics of people with those guns. The good people vs. the bad people, nothing good has come out of them.

Things happen for a reason. There is a hurricane headed towards the Republican Convention in Florida. I take that as a sign from a higher power, whatever you believe in and say hmm... I think that maybe this is a massive sign that someone doesn't want them empowered over us, but that is a guess on my part.

Open your mind and look outside the box. Right now you sit here reading this thinking you liberal idiot, but I dare you to open your mind not to label. I don't believe in Jesus but if everything in that little black book says he was, then he would have been a liberal. Expand what you know with facts and not made up shit you have read in some dumb place. Turn off whatever you read this with and open up a book. You may learn that the ancient ways of doing things make more sense than what is going on in the world today.

I Think and Think

When I think too much, I think way too much. I think, and then I think. I think about things, the things that have me trapped. I think about the way life may have been. I think way too much, I think about the way things should have been. I think and think about the things that have me stuck. I think about the sickness of my life. I think, that I think too much. I think that every little thing needs to be analyzed. I think about what I think about. I think of thinking. Think of thinking is thinking of thought. Then I wander, get lost in a false reality that doesn't exist. The wander is a thought that keeps me thinking. I know that there is no reality to my wanders, they are just thoughts. Think about the wander too much and it will put you in a comatose state of mind and you will fall from reality. Think of the thoughts of falling from this moment. There is no moment that is real, what is real now? Thinking and thoughts have confused the brain and I no longer will figure out reality.

When I think too much, I think excessively. The past is more than a wander thought. The thinking of what has happened to me in the past creates anger or sadness that cannot be filled. I think of the thoughts that I had when I would think in the past and then I think and think and think and think. There is no end to the thoughts of the thinking world and there is no stopping what cannot be controlled. The thoughts of thinking of them drive me insane.

When I think about my future, the thoughts are not pure. I

think that I will forever think about thinking. Thoughts of thinking are controlling my life which makes me happy but also makes me sad. The future I see is one that is made up of thoughts and thinking and thinking and thinking and thoughts from the past and knowing what has happened from the world. I have seen what the world has to offer me and then I begin to think. There is nothing but thoughts. Feet stuck in the depths of the end of the line of thinking. I wander if there will be brain movement after. Though there has to an acceptance of that I will believe in something after the body ends. I think there is. That means that there will be thought of my life throughout from my life and even when I die I will suffer from thinking and there will be no end of the thoughts of the things I have lived. Will I forever suffer from the sorrow of thought or will I be able to separate and become independent? Is there something there waiting in time to make me happy again, but then I will think that it will be there to make me

happy and not really mean anything. Then the thinking

and thinking and thinking and thinking and thinking and

thinking and thinking will never ever fucking end.

Hate Her

Head to the floor

Blood in the carpet

Sadness is over whelming

I couldn't live without you anymore

I made the promise

All would die at my hands

Any that touched you

Then you would be the last, my little whore

There is no God don't beg for what's not there

Jesus is just a moral compass you lost

No special place in the clouds for you

However, I will make sure your body burns

Don't look up and try to pray

You're looking up at the only God you should have

known

Don't fucking beg for your life since it means nothing

now?

I'm the judge, jury, and your fucking Jesus now

Lifeless bodies on the ground surround me

The sirens are in the background and I don't care

I will be the Martyr of your parade for your casket

We will lie beside each other forever like we always

planned

You fucked it all up

You fucking lied

Now you're fucking dead

The blood is on my hands

If I live, I live to pay for your crimes

If I die then I will haunt the others that I couldn't get to

If I live, I live to pay for your crimes

If I die then I will haunt the others that I couldn't get to

No God

No Jesus

No Heaven

No Hell

Just your blood

Past: Realistic Round World Part 1
– Sick, Sick, Sick

I am are diseased in the head

No matter the help

There will not be enough

The mazes that come to rise make me a new Atheist

Sick, Sick in the fucking head

The voices say only dark things

The future that it predicts is grim

When the dark reaches, its hand out there is no hope

In the corner, I try to hide

The shadow casts only evil

There is no moral compass anymore

Jesus has failed God

Sick, Sick in the fucking head

The voices say only dark things

The future that it predicts is grim

When the dark reaches, its hand out there is no hope

Dig at the foundation of what's here

There is no fucking escape from this

Truth hurts and she said I must pay

Mary you forgot to give birth, you failed God

Sick, Sick in the fucking head

The voices say only dark things

The future that it predicts is grim

When the dark reaches, its hand out there is no hope

Time is running out

My fingernails are chewed off

My eyes only cry out blood

My ears ring from the screams

God you forgot to make Heaven and Hell

Sick, Sick in the fucking head

The voices say only dark things

The future that it predicts is grim

When the dark reaches, its hand out there is no hope

It's what you all have said to me

You all meant the world to me

No, No apology will come from me

The evil inside of you is manmade that you created

If there were a God, he would show no mercy on you

Sick, Sick in the fucking head

The voices say only dark things

The future that it predicts is grim

When the dark reaches, its hand out there is no hope

Present: Realistic Round World
Part 2 – You Left Me

Vibrate the energy around me

I found the peace inside of me

I no longer want to be in denial

Cured from her hate

I found you to confide in

You brought the best out in me

The radiance of my Aura was the brightest it has ever

been

Then the new round world ended

All that was found was lost

I found myself confined

All alone in the house

The pup became my best friend

The love I found was through a box

I found you to confide in

You brought the best out in me

The radiance of my Aura was the brightest it has ever

been

Then the new round world ended

All that was found was lost

Television lied because it made me believe

The internet lied because it made me believe

Though I found out that when you push

I pushed through the tunnel and didn't find you

I found you to confide in

You brought the best out in me

The radiance of my Aura was the brightest it has ever

been

Then the new round world ended

All that was found was lost

I would kill for one more shot

I want to go around one more time

The reset button doesn't exist

How I would change everything

I found you to confide in

You brought the best out in me

The radiance of my Aura was the brightest it has ever

been

Then the new round world ended

All that was found was lost

You, You never knew

Maybe, just maybe you knew

Of course, of course you knew

Now , now, I am lost in the walls

I found you to confide in

You brought the best out in me

The radiance of my Aura was the brightest it has ever

been

Then the new round world ended

All that was found was lost

Death: Realistic Round World Part 3 – Astral Travel

Because I found myself not able

She wouldn't let me talk

I hate her for it

Now you're gone and I can't do a thing

I try to sleep to find you

I can't find you in my sleep

I must have upset you

I don't know how to reach you know

I hear the bumps, the cracks, and the footsteps

It could be you watching out over me

I heard a woman's voice the one night

Though I don't think, you would be a dark shadow

I try to sleep to find you

I can't find you in my sleep

I must have upset you

I don't know how to reach you know

Please forgive me for searching

You know that I could always see

Everyone else has come and said goodbye

I never knew that you would leave without stopping by

I try to sleep to find you

I can't find you in my sleep

I must have upset you

I don't know how to reach you know

Where does your energy vibrate?

Where is it that you hide?

There is nothing else out there

Are you just mad at me

I try to sleep to find you

I can't find you in my sleep

I must have upset you

I don't know how to reach you know

Death can't hide you

In this moment

I will vow to find you

She should feel remorse

Keeping me from you

Never said a proper goodbye

Death can't keep me down

I just hope you haven't reincarnated

I try to sleep to find you

I can't find you in my sleep

I must have upset you

I don't know how to reach you know

No, no prayer when there is no God

Pine Box Fire Funeral

It can't be suicide

If you're already dead inside

Emptiness and darkness

It's just a pine box fire funeral

Pour the gasoline

Eyes wide open

The screams can't be heard

Light the match

Robotic actions we all follow

Kneel, sit, stand, Kneel, sit, stand

Think there is sadness when there's not

Emotionless and flat lined in the heart

Pour the gasoline

Eyes wide open

The screams can't be heard

Light the match

The ghost is standing behind you

63

Spirits cry for you

A pine box funeral

It's not suicide if you're dead inside

Pour the gasoline

Eyes wide open

The screams can't be heard

Light the match

Darkness

Nothingness

64

Quietness

Emotionless

Havenless

Helless

The fire has taken the pine box

There is no fear here

It can't be suicide

If you're already dead inside

No Death to meet you

No God like you were taught

No Devil waiting for the spirit

This was your decision

It can't be suicide

If you're already dead inside

Lay to rest alone

An Ode to Staley

No warmth there

Pile on the covers without help

The night will be still and lonely

Put me away in the box

Place me under the bed

If I rattle the cardboard too much and shake the bed

It will be okay to place me in the closet forgotten

I wake fast in the morning thinking someone is there

I rest myself back down as I know there is no one there

The sun is bright and pushes the empty things to do for
the day

The sun takes me out of my only life I have right now

Put me away in the box

Place me under the bed

If I rattle the cardboard too much and shake the bed

It will be okay to place me in the closet forgotten

Nowhere to go in the morning

No hurry up out the door

No motivation to move and go

No more sitting thinking about the past, present, and future

Put me away in the box

Place me under the bed

If I rattle the cardboard too much and shake the bed

It will be okay to place me in the closet forgotten

I have learned who is here

I have learned who is not

Good friends have come and some very close have gone

Not sure, what I have done to place me in this situation

Put me away in the box

Place me under the bed

If I rattle the cardboard too much and shake the bed

It will be okay to place me in the closet forgotten

Stir crazy pacing away

Trolling the computer like a mad man

Watching every movie known

Still I cannot walk out my door to anyone

Put me away in the box

Place me under the bed

If I rattle the cardboard too much and shake the bed

It will be okay to place me in the closet forgotten

This is no one's fault but my own

I didn't want to lose anyone in all of this

My path led me to things I didn't expect

The sun has fallen and I can't feel the energy I felt before

Put me away in the box

Place me under the bed

If I rattle the cardboard too much and shake the bed

It will be okay to place me in the closet forgotten

10 ½ Pills

One was hard

Two was easier

However, now I have no one but the walls

Year by year brings me closer to the end

I see friends come and go

Relationships they just go

Friends I find in boxes with flowers around them

I am half way at the end

Pushed and shoved by the evil that has placed me in these walls

They say Karma will get her in the end

How can you buy your way into Heaven when there is no God

Get down from your soapbox and lay in the dirt where you belong

I see friends come and go

Relationships they just go

Friends I find in boxes with flowers around them

I am half way at the end

Too many factors have put me here

I blame the world for the injustices that have been caused

However, the walls get closer and closer

I take another pill to push them back again

I see friends come and go

Relationships they just go

Friends I find in boxes with flowers around them

I am half way to the end

Another prescribed pill by the doctors

Some for my heart

Others for the stress

A few that keeps me from destroying all of you

I see friends come and go

Relationships they just go

Friends I find in boxes

I am halfway to my box with flowers around it

Double Edge Sword

How can I be unhappy when I have everything but the past?

When will I get forgiven in my mind to be happy within?

I feel like I need to scream all the time.

I am one of the luckiest people in the world.

Inside I feel dead and lacking something.

When can I see the world as I did once before?

Why can't I just be happy with what I have?

Does there have to be more?

Is this all there is for me?

Work...Sleep...Work...Sleep...

Double edge sword should have me happy when I am

dying inside.

I know I can't erase the past and can only move forward.

I have learned from the past.

I fucked up the past.

I have a new beginning.

And almost a fresh start.

However, sleep continues to be my best friend...

In the House

Well normally, I wait to get depressed from listening to music and the pills to kick in before I poor my guts out but I am going to before that happens. I am all ready for things I don't need the additives to help. I haven't written in a while because I moved into a house away from everyone and am now committed for 30 years or less depending on my payment skills. I have a pile of trash in my dining room that is a monster. That doesn't bring me here though. The broken toilet that I have fixed three times now does not bring me here. A dog that wakes me the sleeper up every day at seven AM isn't the reason I am here. Waiting over a week for cable and internet doesn't bring me here. The car that is complicated in and out of state does not bring me here.

I have found myself figuring out things that I should have figured out years ago. This is an adventure that I have always wanted to do with someone else. In fact, I did do that. Now I look back on everything from then and now, the pills that I take, and the people I see, to pretend that I am normal, it all brings me back to here. It doesn't matter how close you are, you are miles away. Bless those that have tried, the ones that have shown love, it has always been me.

When I was sixteen, I moved from my mother's to my dad's. It started then if not before. The grass isn't greener and life is hard. I can't make myself not be in a funk, either I am or I am not. When I was twenty, I moved back into my mothers, and then into a relationship. From there to

Pittsburgh with my friends, never settling down I drank myself to oblivion until I realized at least that alcohol is bad, it truly is.

I can blame alcohol and depression on hereditary but the women in my life I can't. I have hurt too many women and can't even look most in the eyes. The mistakes I will live within for now in this big house alone, inside my head.

Nightly Thoughts

How many people have I hurt? Many have lain beside me,
then things went wrong, and then I left. I'm a nice person
who seems to finish last. Though last means that I have
fucked up others' lives. I do not know how others live with
my mistakes and I lay in bed nightly thinking about all of
them.

If I messed up your life, I am sorry. My brain aches every
night. My soul hurts. No doctor can fix me, just medicate. I
am a zombie that still feels. I feel and urn for someone to

hold me in my bed at night, to tell me everything is going to be all right.

The things that went wrong in my life have put me on a great path, but in the end if there is no one then there is nothing. The things in my head may be wrong, they be right. If there is a difference in thought, don't let me know, my soul will cry.

I need nothing from anyone, but want everything. No matter where I go I will continue until I find someone to deal with my crazy, lazy, aching, and medicated ass. I can't see anyone who can, but I dream of someone who can.

These are my thoughts every night. When I lay down to sleep.

Morpheus

What I lack at times brings me to rage, but then there is times where I am just impatient. The impatient part is what gets me more than anything does. I don't know why I find certain things calming but want to jump into someone sometimes. That's why I take a pill and then another to help it, it's like two or three maybe four.

Though the one makes wired and energetic for the day and I take it before I go before bed with two others that make me sleep so now I just lay there in bed bouncing back and forth until I pick up my phone and play songs or a game.

Lord of sleep Morpheus, where are you sometimes. I should be in bed right now but I never even lay down. I didn't even try. Maynard is out and has been for two hours. To sleep like a dog, would it be great, living most of your life in dream?

My back hurts and I am listening to Hurt and I don't want to lie down but I know Maynard will wake at 730. How people with "crumb snatchers" (To The Late Hollywood) live? I don't think I could do it...
It might be why I destroy every relationship I am in, or I am an asshole. The poles haven't come back yet but I'll go with a dead heat.

So, 1, 2, take some pills, 3, 4, take some more and

tomorrow you may be normal...

Perceptive Muteness Shifts Us Onward

Not voices, not words, not descriptions, just knowing.

Third eye, voice, or knowledge without knowing.

I know your fate before of you knowing.

It is what I am, the all-knowing.

It just pops in my head as if already knowing.

It screams in silence.

It sends vibrations through my mind in silence.

I want to reject the silence.

Just for it to speak instead of staying in silence.

It is never wrong even in its energetic silence.

This thing cannot hold me still, it moves.

In my own heart, it makes it skip a beat when it moves.

Down my body to my feet from my mind it moves.

Hands to my head it takes me to the ground as it moves.

I accept the things that I know as the world moves.

It knows what will become of us.

It knows those things that no one else knows about us.

Out and Out Fervor

Blue sky, tall trees on the mountaintops, and the bluest water in the valley that anyone has ever seen. Deer and small critters run through the forest of the greenest trees with eagles flying high above. They run and fly to the bluest water and drink from the calm slow moving river. However, I am not in this place.

I find myself in orange sand in the middle of a dessert with the wind whipping me in the face. The sky is not blue; it is the darkest shade of red that is unimaginable. A road is looking to be a worn path. In both directions, it leads to nowhere. I know because I have traveled down them both but they lead me back to the same place.

A spade shovel is sticking out of the ground. Out of instinct, I know what to do. I start to dig. Why do I dig? Is there a reason? What am I going to find in this hole? Am I digging my own last resting place? However, I find myself not digging straight down like a grave. The digging seems like it takes forever for whatever I am digging. However, where I am, it seems to have no time. I stop and look at my progress and I have not realized that I have dug a four by four foot hole four feet down.

Lobbing my shovel out to the road and it clangs off something. Nothing should be there but the beaten down path. I turn and look and I find cinder blocks stacked as if I were to make a foundation for something. The hole I have dug seems like it would be perfect for the amount that is stacked in a perfect square. I climb out of the hole and look around and around but there is no one in sight. There has never been anyone in sight here.

One block by another block, I toss them into the foundation hole. I throw as many as the hole can fit with much more to follow. I jump down and start laying them out along the evenly dug out walls. The walls are even and the placement of each block works out perfectly. I work the entire way around and begin again. Tossing and tossing more block into the foundation I realize that once again I have no idea how much time I have spent here. My muscles are sore. I have blisters on my hands. My knees are scraped up and bleeding some. However, I jump back in.

Resetting the blocks from the first row, I go around the walls that have been perfectly dug by my blistered hands. The third row goes around and around and rows grow and grow offset from the last. Finally, I run out of block. I stand and look at my accomplishment, what I have bleed and sweet over for an unimaginable amount of time. The dust starts to push hard and begins to fill up the center and I begin to panic. I look back for my shovel and there sits a perfect stack of wood, just like the blocks.

I hear thunder claps in the background from all directions around me. I feel drops of liquid and I reach out my hand. It is black raindrops falling from the cloudless sky. I realize that I must work fast to make, to make, to make a shed? It appears to have everything I need two by fours and plywood. There is a bucket of nails and with a hammer lying on top.

Lifting a plank of wood and I throw it to one side and then another side. To even it out to make things easy because the ground was turning from dry dusty sand to wet black tar ground that made moving around difficult. I grab my bucket to get started by grabbing the first piece of wood, which happened to be the perfect size to the foundation. The construction of the floor moved fast because I had to move fast. Winds quickly moving through my area making the tar rain blow sideways straight in my face. At a certain point, I had to begin to feel around and hammer nails by faith in myself.

With the studs in place, I picked up a piece of plywood. The wind blew me around and down the path. All I could do is hang on with lightning blasting beside me as I rode the ply wood back to the stack of wood in front of the shed. A never-ending loop continues to exist in the orange wasteland of nothingness. With the wind still at a high, I slide the first piece of plywood slowly, inch by inch to the studded flooring. I nail that beast to the studs all the way down. Again, it all came to a perfect fit.

I stand up but a gust of wet orange-blackened sand knocks me over. This makes me crawl for the second piece of plywood that would finish the floor. Again, I crawl and move the plywood inch by inch, on what is to be ground. Making it there, I hurry to nail down the floor so I do not take another ride down the dusty path. The wind stops with the last nail connecting plywood to the stud. I look up to the

cloudless dark red sky and the black rain has
stopped as well.

In this moment of calmness I look at myself to look
to see how badly I am hurt. I have scraps on my
arms and my forehead has lumps from it banging off
the flying plywood. My back and legs are killing me
and my clothing ripped. I can feel a black eye
developing, but at least for now, I can see. I look
and I wonder how I am going to move and make
walls with the wood while realizing I do not have
enough wood for a roof.

I crawl up from the flooring and start to grab the wood and again throwing it where I need it. I realize at this point that I have no door either. I do not understand what I am supposed to do with the missing parts. The struggles ahead are going to be hard. However, I work through the struggles of pain and time lose and no thoughts running through my mind, just one objective, and use the tool given to me.

I put up the first, the second, third, and on the fourth even without a door, the wood is already perfectly cut to place a doorframe. There are no plans. There is no thought in my head on how I am building just randomly, but I am winging it. I take a step back and look at the structure. It comes to me. It is a room. The doorframe is for a regular door not a shed door. However, I am out of materials, I cannot go on. I look up at the sky and wonder why I have been through this torture. Then it hits me I turn around and there lay the materials to make the roof and a ladder.

Without haste, I grab one truss and I begin to construct the roof. The trusses do not take long then I grab the plywood and nail it to the trusses.

There was no roofing paper or shingles. I look down at the path and there they lay. I climb down grab the first roll, cut relay, and cut repeatedly. I start grabbing packs of shingles and place them on the roof. Once everything is on top, I rip open the packs and begin the long tediousness of shingling a roof. One side done, with the first time excitement is growing. I peak down at the path and it has the door and the hinges on it. Once done, I fly down the ladder that disappears once I am down and walking away. I do not care where it went I am almost done.

I grab the hinges and screw them into place. I grab the door, place the door on the hinges, and close it. I take a step back and look at the room in the middle of nowhere that I have made. Bruised, beaten by the elements, and tortured by continues work without knowledge of time, I am done. Done, there is not a thing going to connect to this room. All becomes quite for the first time. No blowing orange sand, claps of thunder, only the sound of a piece of wood hitting the beaten path behind me.

Fear full of my body and what could be next I slowly turn around and find an ornamental wooded

103

plaque with letters inscribed in it. I cannot read from where I am but I am scared of what the carving says. Slowly I make the full turn and step slowly inch by inch with fear creeping heavily into my mind. I get to the plague and it has writing on it that I cannot understand. I pick it up and stare at it. There are two screws on top of it, so I take over the plaque to the room and screw it onto the door.

Even with all this, I still have no idea why my instincts have lead me here to do all of this. I grab the door handle and open it. I hear another sound of wood hitting the ground and then another and then another. Three pieces of wood in total, I turn and they are shelves for the room. What am I going to do with shelves in the middle of nowhere in an endless and seemingly hopeless wasteland? Though, like before I grab them and there again out of instinct just walk into this room and hang them where I feel they should be hung.

I walk out and shut the door. For the first time I feel complete. Though the weather again is picking up and the wind is really blowing hard, I look around and see lightning and there it was a tornado. I run to the room to let myself in but I cannot get in.

The room will not let me. I run to the opposite side

of the room that I created and know that it is not

tornado proof. I can hear the roar from it and the

all the orange sand starts to fly up and around me.

I close my eyes and wait for death. Death had other

plans though that day.

I stood by pushing myself up using the room and

walked around to the front and the path is still

there unharmed the vast emptiness of orange ugly

desert still exists. Limping now I walk to the path

and look at the room, it was unharmed. However,

something catches my eye to the left of the room. There are more foundations. There are plaques lying charred and what looks to be a burnt floor. Is this a place where others have been sent for some unknown punishable reason?

I slowly limp over to the ruins of the old foundations and look down at the plaque. This name was a woman's name, a name that I recognize, I do not understand. I walk to another and the same thing. I look at all the plaques and they all have women's names that I know. I turn and look at the room that I built and limp to it as fast as I can get to it. Her name, her name is here. I open the door

and all the memories and mementoes are all on the

shelves and pictures of us on the shelves. I left her

in like the others, inside. I walked out, closed the

door, and looked at the name on the door. Looking

down I see a gas can and a lighter on top.

Fairy Tale: Down, Down, Down, Down

Once upon a time, I believed

I believed until I found the way

The secrets of the past became clear

All shall know the dirt you lay in now

Down, Down, Down, Down

On your knees in front of the bed

He cannot help you now

All hope is gone for you now

Not even he wants you

You can try to stand on the highest peak

Reach toward the sky

Try to find something to grab onto

Do not let the sun melt your wings

On your knees in front of the bed

He cannot help you now

All hope is gone for you now

Not even, he wants you

Down, Down, Down, Down

Try to find your way by moving around

Person to person, on your knees in front of them

Still you find the emptiness inside

That is because you fill empty holes with fairy tales

On your knees in front of the bed

He cannot help you now

All hope is gone for you now

Not even, he wants you

Fairy tales do not exist

No mystical animal is here to help you

No man on a white horse is here

No rabbit is going to show you down a hole

No man on a torture symbol is going to come back and

save you

On your knees sucking his dick will not help

He refuses to see you as a person now

All your hope is gone from him

Take your bow and end this tale

Down, Down, Down, Down

Just six feet

Laying on your back again

Looking up at darkness like every other night

Down, Down, Down, Down

20.8.5.18.5_9.19_14.15_7.15.4_8.5.18.8_ 46.774201.23.516407

Window Watcher of Twenty-two

Where are the people going?

They all drive on the highway to go somewhere.

I watch from my window.

The great highway twenty-two moves everyone around.

Where do they all go?

Is there somewhere to be?

Why can't I go where they are going?

Fucking left inside looking out the windows!

Does my existence mean nothing to the world?

Fuck them, I don't need them.

Go speeding past in your little cars.

Left behind here that is nowhere to all of them.

It's fine I like that you leave me alone.

I make better company than anyone else.

Is there somewhere to be?

Why can't I go where they are going?

Fucking left inside looking out the windows!

Does my existence mean nothing to the world?

Is it that you are going to see someone?

Do you have family that you are seeing?

Is there someone you are meeting that you love?

Are the two of you going to fuck?

Why did you leave me looking out?

Is there somewhere to be?

Why can't I go where they are going?

Fucking left inside looking out the windows!

Does my existence mean nothing to the world?

How many people out there are happy?

Is there any that are sad?

How many people are doing the same thing right now?

You go speeding past my life and me.

Did you find yourself at a dead end?

Is there somewhere to be?

Why can't I go where they are going?

Fucking left inside looking out the windows!

Does my existence mean nothing to the world?

Are you at the end of the road?

117

Do you find yourself alone?

Do you expect me to pick you up now?

Not again, I do not care

I do not give a fuck about you or the others that drove

past.

In between states, here and there, one road to travel, do

you think about the people that you pass?

Is there somewhere to be?

Why can't I go where they are going?

Fucking left inside looking out the windows!

Does my existence mean nothing to the world?

Jump off either fucking bridge.

Jump off into the cold water.

Jump off for driving pass me.

Jump off for not caring about the people you pass up.

Jump off for not stopping or giving a shit!

Is there somewhere to be?

Why can't I go where they are going?

Fucking left inside looking out the windows!

119

Does my existence mean nothing to the world?

Where did all the people go?

No one is out there anymore.

Cars spaced going here and there.

All the cars have their lights on.

Everyone must be home in bed and forgotten about the

window watcher.

This is what I have done, emptiness, hopelessness, and

driven everyone to twenty-two.

Is there somewhere to be?

Why can't I go where they are going?

Fucking left inside looking out the windows!

Does my existence mean nothing to the world?

It's where I have placed myself.

In a hole, I dug myself in.

This is not my fault.

Blind

The tires stop and the breaks make a slight squealing sound at the bottom of the hill. Three doors open in the dark overcast damp night of the car. Three people get out settling their boots on the wet cement. Two adults and one child of an early age get out of the old car. All three close their door but do so without making a sound. They stand there still for a moment in the same attire, each with long trench coats with a hood that is pulled over their head. The hoods come over the top of their head so much so that their faces are unseen. The sleeves of these leather coats go down and almost cover all their hands except the fingers. The fingers and the rest of the hands are covers by leather gloves that make the sound of leather stretching every time they move their hands or even their bodies from their coats. What is on underneath is unknown. Though you can tell, that one adult is female and the other is male by the shape of their figures. Both are of equal height and the child comes up to their waste and is unknown of the gender or age of the child.

All three walk over to the sidewalk and step up onto it. All you hear is the leather stretching with every small movement. The three turn towards a house they have parked in front of, the home is not theirs. The origin of the owners is unknown to the three as they walk towards the home. All the lights are out in this normal suburban home. There are homes that are similar the entire way up the hill and all their lights are out as well.

It is very late at night and the three stand on the cement porch with the child in front and the adults stand behind the child frozen as the child knocks on the door. There is nothing at first and then the child rings the doorbell. A light turns on. You can hear people talking inside wondering who would ring the bell at three in the morning. You can hear the pad locks open up and the doorknob turn. The door slowly opens with little light shining through the open space in the door. A man stands there, looks at the three, and does not say a word and neither does the three. The man opens the door wide, steps to the side, lets the three in, and closes the door behind them.

There is no sound from the house. There are no conversations that could be heard. There is no commotion. Everything is peaceful and calm. It would appear that the three were known members of the family or friends of those that occupy the house. All the lights turn off in the house and still silence throughout the neighborhood. The house and only that house begin to shake slightly as if in a small earthquake but it was only their earthquake. No other house moved up the hill. All stayed silent throughout the over casted damp night. Then a light appears in the house. It seems to start in the middle and grows brighter and brighter but slowly. It is as if it is taking its time going over everything and everyone in the house until the light is so bright it is like looking into the sun and then there is darkness.

The door opens up, the child walks out, and then each adult after. They walk to their car and to each ones respected door and stands there for a moment like when they did when they removed themselves from the car. Simultaneously they slowly open the car doors, look up at the hill at the other houses, and then sit in the car closing the doors without a sound. The car starts up. The first sound since the car had stopped. With the engine ready, the car slowly pulls forward releasing the breaks and the tires rolling over the damp concrete. The car moves quietly and slowly up the hill and following the road into the forest at the end of the neighborhood and disappears.

Later as the sun comes out and removes the dampness along with the clouds. Everyone begins to move about and start his or her day. The paperboy delivers the newspaper to every house. People slowly go out and crab it off their perfectly manicured lawns or front steps. A local resident does not pick up his newspaper. The house that had the visitors from early in the morning was the only one left with a newspaper. The neighbor notices it, walks over to the house, picks up the paper, and knocks on his neighbor's door. The man notices no noises, no sounds, no commotion of children or the sound of talking.

The neighbor becomes concerned and starts beating on the door and ringing the doorbell. The man knows something is wrong. The owner of this house is very prompt, never misses the paper and makes sure his family is up early every day to enjoy it. He begins to start going around and knocking on windows and looking in but sees no one or anything out of place. His wife yells out to him to inquire if there is something wrong. The man instructs his wife to go to the phone and get the operator to get the police over to the house immediately. The wife does as instructed and it is not long before two officers in one squad car arrive at the house.

The neighbor greats them and tells the officers that there must be something wrong and that they must help the people inside. The officers agree and knock on the door and then ring the doorbell. They split into two as one goes to the back and checks things out from back there. The other officer stays in the front of the house, looks in the windows, and sees a normal well-kept house with no one inside. The

officers meet back up in the front and agree they
have enough to force the door open and search the
house.

They try just using their shoulder but it seems like
the doors dead bolts still locked. The neighbor
reassures the officers that they are doing the right
thing. The slightly bigger of the two men uses all
his force and kicks in the front door. They yell for
the family and begin the search of the house. The
dead bolt was indeed still locked; in fact, everything
from the inside was still locked. They check every
room including the closets and under the beds,
there was simply no one in the house. The house
was empty even the car were still there.

The officers begin to ask other neighbors that had
walked down the hill questions. Had they seen the

family recently? Most said they seen them the day before and couldn't understand where they could of gone without their car. The officers had to turn the home into a crime scene and call in detectives that went house to house asking questions and inspecting the home. Nothing made sense to the officers or the detectives. They declared the family missing and left the home of the missing family into as a crime scene.

Darkness fell onto the suburban hillside without a cloud in the sky. However, there were many concerns for the missing family. Talk amongst the neighbors started and all made sure to lock their doors and windows as a precaution. However, nothing would happen again for several nights. The officers would cruise by at night to check up on the hillside but nothing turned up or the family. It came to the point that the neighbors had given up hope and stopped wondering where the missing family had gone to. The entire neighborhood started to forget and so did the officers. Fewer cruise by drives at night until there was none and the house at the bottom of the hill had just become an empty home.

Three months had passed when a black older looking car drove up to the house next to the empty house. It was a damp and cloudy night like before. Like before, three doors opened and the same figures arouse from the car. The doors closed silently and the three walked up to the home of the man that had first noticed the other family missing. All was dark and no one had a light on, as it was three in the morning again. The child reached up and rang the doorbell and the man that first noticed slowly opened the door and looked at the three. The man did not say a single word as he stepped to the side and let the three inside of his home.

The hillside silent damp and over casted with many clouds would once again have its own earthquake for just one house. As the house shook the light from the center of the house grew bigger and bigger. The light became unbearable to look at like before. Then without a noise, the light vanished and the three walked outside into the darkness and moved to the car. The three stood there with their respective doors open as they looked up the hillside. No one had awakened; all was still dark and quiet. The three slipped back in their car and closed the door in silence. The automobile had been started up and crawled up the hill slowly and drove into the woods.

The next day the delivery boy delivered the newspaper to all the houses except one. Everyone began their day by going out to get their newspapers to read and start the day. The next-door neighbor of the house that had their paper still on the sidewalk looked around and began to worry. Like the other neighbors that disappeared this was not normal. He ran over to the house dropping his coffee cup with it shattering on the cement. It was like before. No one answered the doors. The officers and detectives came and knocked down the door and the house was spotless. All the locks shut from inside and the car was still there.

Over the next few nights, people started to panic and wondered if they would be next. People of the hillside began to go and stay with their parents, friends or just left. They tried to sell their homes but no one wanted to buy in that neighborhood. The entire town had become spooked of that area and never traveled up there. The people that were stuck had started a neighborhood watch though for months nothing happened. Each would take turns with a shotgun and walk up and down the hillside watching and waiting. However, nothing came and then the neighborhood watch turned into watch out your window with a gun near. Then again, people forgot about the people that had disappeared or talked about it to the towns' folk as if it was a fairytale horror movie.

On one dark cloudy night with the dampness in the air, a car drove up on to the hillside three months from when the last family was taken. However, the car did not stop at the next house because no one lived there anymore. It did not stop either at the next house either as that family had also moved. The car finally stopped on the sixth house. This time was different. There was a light on.

However, the three still opened their car doors and stepped out of the vehicle. With the leather making the stretching sound as they stood and looked up at the hillside and seen that most people were gone. All three simultaneously closed the doors silently and walked to the house that they had parked at. The child reached up and rang the doorbell. A commotion started inside the house yelling started.

The voice from inside demanded to know who they were and what they were doing there at three in the morning. He left them know that he had a gun. From a side window, he peered outside and could see the three that stood there in front of his door. He demanded that they show there face or he would start shooting at them even the child. The three complied and simultaneously reached above their heads and grabbed the top of the hoods that covered half of their faces making it impossible to be seen. They turned their head, faced him without turning their bodies, and removed the hoods. The face that the man was expecting to see was not there. There was no woman, man, or child. They did not even have faces but a skull like structure without eyes, nose holes, ears, or a mouth. There was just light grey skin that covered their entire face. Then they looked forward again.

The door opened up and there was the man with his gun. He did not shoot and did not say a single word. The man left them in with silence filling the damp air. Then the house that the three entered began to shake silently on the hillside just like the others. With a light starting to overtake, the home like the others to the brightness of the sun and then went dark. Everything was still once again.

The three walked out and went to the car with their hoods up over their heads. They stopped at the car door and looked up at the hillside and then they looked down and towards the town. They looked at each other and realized that people had awakened to the sound of the man screaming. The people stood there not knowing what to do. There was a siren in the background and the three sat in the car and drove up into the woods like always but this time with people watching.

When the police arrived, what was left of the neighborhood tried to tell them what they saw but the officers did not understand no faced grey-skinned people, violently shaking a house, and omitting a sun like light. They inspected the latest family's home and found the same thing like always. Locked doors, windows, and a car still left inside the garage. The detectives interviewed the people repeatedly but they could not understand how a family of three with a child could do any harm to three families of six on this hillside. To the detectives it was impossible.

After that night, the hillside neighborhood decided to move before the family visited again. The hill became vacant and the houses torn down and a memorial park with a children's playground in remembrance of the twelve children that had disappeared. To the town the story just became a legend of something that was just an old folklore in time.

Wine into Water

I do not look like you,

I do not dress like you,

My music plays differently than yours,

I inked up my arms,

I do not want to be like you.

Did I fuck up your life?

I didn't realize everything hinged on the matters of three,

Missed your youth like I did,

Pissed it all away on drugs and cigarettes,

I stopped caring about two stone slabs a long time ago,

One life, no many lives,

Feeling inside make my eyes bleed,

Do not pretend you are little miss perfect,

Drink from the cup on your knees,

No wait it is wine that is supposed to be in there.

Just like kin to be like other kin,

Follow the false morality rules,

Pick up that fucking stone,

Throw it, throw more, and kill him!

Here is the gasoline and the lighter fluid,

Repent and join reality before you are completely lost,

Here is the match,

One last time to bend down,

Burn the manmade book of control and disorder.

Did I fuck up your life?

I didn't realize everything hinged the matters of three,

Missed your youth like I did,

Pissed it all away on drugs and cigarettes,

I stopped caring about two stone slabs a long time ago,

No one forced marriage,

No one forced the birth,

Now all you do is blame,

Now all you want is Jesus,

However, he is not there,

However, there is no God to repent to either,

143

You are going to lose your trinity.

Atramentous Elliptic

Atramentous elliptic in the evening sky,

Fly over the world,

Goes forever and disappears,

There was an atramentous elliptic above us.

Wake up in the middle of the night,

I wake to not being on my bed,

Find myself unattached in the air,

I realize of the acclivity and fall to the bed.

It took two to see,

Only one would admit to seeing,

No reports filed,

Jet shook my house.

Wake up in the middle of the night,

I wake to not being on my bed,

Find myself unattached in the air,

I realize of the acclivity and fall to the bed.

I want to know where I have been,

I want to hide from it all,

Was I just another experiment?

The things that I could have seen,

I want to hide from it all!

146

Wake up in the middle of the night,

I wake to not being on my bed,

Find myself unattached in the air,

I realize of the acclivity and fall to the bed.

My head races with images in my head,

Am I insane or just lost in my imagination?

Flashing through the moments,

Do I deserve to know?

Can I comprehend what is going on?

Wake up in the middle of the night,

I wake to not being on my bed,

Find myself unattached in the air,

I realize of the acclivity and fall to the bed.

Was I sent back with a purpose?

Is there something I am to do?

Why won't you let me remember?

I deserve to know everything!

Wake up in the middle of the night,

I wake to not being on my bed,

Find myself unattached in the air,

I realize of the acclivity and fall to the bed,

I sweat from fear,

Am I going to the end?

Is death near or are you just close?

Give me the answers so I can sleep at night!

Wake up in the middle of the night,

I wake to not being on my bed,

Find myself unattached in the air,

I realize of the acclivity and fall to the bed.

Un Outil Parfait

Let me know everything is going to be okay.

Hold me tight as I cry and squeeze you closer.

Do not go away from me until I am no longer scared.

Stay here and keep rubbing my head with your fingernails.

I stand outside my body looking at the world.

I see myself acting in a way that even I am surprised.

I hear the voice telling me what to do.

I always do what it says.

When I see through my eyes, the damage has been done.

Now I have to fix the things that I did as I watched.

The things I do I have never been able to stop.

It has been like this since I can remember anything.

I watch myself create these acts.

I can see why people think I am an ass.

I see me manipulate everything I want.

I always get the voices what they want.

It takes time but I will see again through the tears.

This was not how I thought things would be.

These things should have never of happened.

However, I made these things happen.

I wonder is there separation between the voices and me.

I wonder if I control it somehow with my mind.

I think I have gone too far this time.

I have crushed another person and then that is when the voice wins.

It likes to put me in situations to control you.

The voice will take everything from you.

There is not a limit of deceit.

Controlling you and controlling me, every time.

I cannot regain control until I runaway.

I then sit and think about what has happened.

I wonder if I can ever come back from what the voice has done.

I just wish for a little while it would be silent in my head.

When I try to sleep, it is controlling my dreams.

Everything it puts in my dreams, dictates my emotion for the day.

Control is lost in translation of the hours the longer I am awake.

Work, home, rest, vacation, and sleep it never stops.

I wonder if I am blessed.

I wonder if the things I have done is for a greater purpose.

I wish I knew if I could gain complete control.

I long for the day when I stop hurting.

One to another to another I go for comfort.

The people I meet are my victims.

All the things the voice says to do to you is only a matter of time.

There is no fighting it, so you might as well play along.

I will manipulate you.

I will control everything around us.

I will dictate your life and mine.

I will make you mine.

I will cage you like a rat.

I will poke a stick at the snake.

I will get bored.

I will leave you wondering what happened to your life.

I will disappear and destroy everything around you.

I will tear your heart to shreds.

I will feel remorse when I am alone at night.

I will want to listen to the other half that you held.

I will want to be that other half.

I will want to stop the hurt, the voice will never stop, and it lives in this moment.

There is a real me inside.

It comes out occasionally.

Loving, caring, the emotion, the feeling, and the tenderness are real.

However, it will continue in its perfect circle of destruction.

I am truly sorry for the past, present, and what will happen in the future.

I am just its tool of deception.

Stay away...

23 hours 56 minutes and 4 seconds

Nine hundred and thirteen miles per hour

Just one person

A place that does not matter

No one around for days

Spinning counter clockwise

One speak of dust

Somewhere without anyone else

No human interaction for weeks

Three hundred and eighty-four kilometers from the dark
side

No one knows you are even there

Invisible to everything

Extraterrestrial contact only for months

One hundred million kilometers from the light

Scream for no one to hear you

Mother Nature no longer acknowledges your existence

The light is bright through the windows only at night

Five hundred and eighty-five miles to go nowhere

Needs of human emotion will eat at you

Fallen off the radar from people

They will not take me away

Periapsis is the shortest distance bringing sadness

Human urges will have you reconsider everything

No one knows you are alive

More tests just take me somewhere else

Aphelion the longest distance away and it brings happiness

Things you never considered before you begin to consider

You at times wish that you were dead

There is another place take me there

Nine point eight meters per second squared keeps us here

The urge of human contact begins to erupt

You wonder what will be said at your eulogy

Find me goldilocks in another area

One point six meters per second squared on our neighbor

You think and plan on how to accomplish the goal

Will your casket be open or closed

Take me away Grey's

Twelve month cycle, thirty-three years ago made metal

Then you take your medicine and sit back down

The casket will all depend on how your energy leaves

I watch the news for your appearances

Twenty-six thousand Before Common Era there was
Yellow

You will start tomorrow and repeat

Six feet down is where your vessel will lay

One day you will take me home where I belong

Twenty-four hours and three hundred and sixty four and
a half

Nothing can ever be the same from back then

You will haunt whomever you want

Where is it out there that I do belong?

Little Legs

(Based on true events)

Born into this world with six

My life is chasing after the sixth

Awake or asleep I know you're there

When you're gone you're really not

Why are you no longer by my bedside?

The dreams awake me to you being there

You find your way to follow me everywhere

Why did you have to hit me?

Little legs running through the hallway

Birthday balloon floating around with no one holding it

Dishes crashing out of cabinets

Knocking at the door with no one there

Where is the one who showed me the sixth?

Standing at the end of the bed waiting

Nowhere to go but to stand around and watch

Phone rings with someone in the house being the only one there

Music and parties in the living room

Pushing me at night

Leaving a hand mark on my thigh

Knowing Death is close here

Little legs running through the hallway

Birthday balloon floating around with no one holding it

Dishes crashing out of cabinets

Knocking at the door with no one there

Out with old friends

A cut forms up my arm and begins to bleed

I see all of you around in the bar

Lost souls stuck for another drink

There is a man made of fur

I have never seen him

Though two close to me have

Looking out over me or torturing me

Little legs running through the hallway

Birthday balloon floating around with no one holding it

Dishes crashing out of cabinets

Knocking at the door with no one there

Knowing that you are there

Sixth lets me see what you look like

You feed off me and have me do your bidding

Though I know this I will continue on

Go here and go there

We look for others in places that are known

Field trips all around to feed the sixth

Though there are doubters but I help them anyway

Little legs running through the hallway

Birthday balloon floating around with no one holding it

Dishes crashing out of cabinets

Knocking at the door with no one there

Finding others in my sleep

Relatives search me out to converse

Sleeping I can slip between realms

However, I try to find others as well

There is energy around every living thing

All different colors of the rainbow

The Death Aura is real and I have seen it

There is no magical golden palace awaiting you in the
clouds

Little legs running through the hallway

Birthday balloon floating around with no one holding it

Dishes crashing out of cabinets

Knocking at the door with no one there

The curse is strong...

Impatient Therapy

Lay beside me

Find me under the covers

Grab me up in your arms

Pull me tight

I want to know what it's like to feel safe

I want to know what love is again

Where are you my sweet love?

An empty bed is always cold without you

Have I ever loved?

These emotions that I have felt

Not sure what is real and what is fake

Time is running together and I am growing older

I want to know what it's like to feel safe

I want to know what love is again

Where are you my sweet love?

An empty bed is always cold without you

Life is passing me by

Friends and relatives have moved forward

I stand still watching the world move

All I want is the feeling of time to stop

I want to know what it's like to feel safe

I want to know what love is again

Where are you my sweet love?

An empty bed is always cold without you

Stop moving around me

Let me find you out of the crowd

However, I can't because I won't look

I am scared to try again

I want to know what it's like to feel safe

I want to know what love is again

Where are you my sweet love?

An empty bed is always cold without you

I don't want to hurt you but I will

I will find a way to push you away

I can't let you be a casualty

I must let you go to save your life

I am now alone

I want to know what it's like to feel safe

I want to know what love is again

Where are you my sweet love?

An empty bed is always cold without you

In the corner in a dark room

All the mirrors are covered up

The windows are darkened

Muttering and crying to myself

Answering my own questions

I want to know what it's like to feel safe

I want to know what love is again

Where are you my sweet love?

An empty house is always cold without you

However, you creep back in slowly

Little things at the beginning

Like trying to get a wounded animal out of hiding

The dark has changed me and made me weak

You lift me up and drag me to bed

Lay me down

You cuddle up against me

Pull the covers up and hold me tight

I cry and cry over and over again

You try to make feel like it's safe

You want to know what love is again

You my sweet love are here

An empty life is always cold without you

Rejuvenation

See you lay in your bed from the glass

In the air through the crack in your window

At the end of the bed and gaze

Asleep alone cover disheveled

In the darkness of the night

Lurking above you face to face

Violate the dreams that run a long in your dream

Hold you down and take what I want

Never knew about anything about the night

Drained all day from the night before

The first time is a test to see if you would wake

Time will tell when it will happen to you again

Weakness has set in and it is time for a visit

Watching waiting for you to hit that deep sleep

When you are gone is when it will happen again

Then you are asleep and the air brings things face to face

In the darkness of the night

Lurking above you face to face

Violate the dreams that run a long in your dream

Hold you down and take what I want

Each time it happens you get drained further

Every time the aura is touched

Anytime the fields of matter are close

Slowly making you mine

Visits come often

We grow closer and closer

The connection is tightly bounded

Manipulations of your dreams are pleasure

In the darkness of the night

Lurking above you face to face

Violate the dreams that run a long in your dream

Hold you down and take what I want

Mind fucking night after night

You are slowly growing in love

You awake tired but feeling emotional

Being inside brings joy when it is in both places

Your mind and your vagina is mine

Soon you will do whatever I want

You are in love with me yet I was never here

Getting fucked and you wonder who it is with

In the darkness of the night

Lurking above you face to face

Violate the dreams that run a long in your dream

Hold you down and take what I want

Tonight, tonight, tonight

All shall be merged together

Mind fucking and raped

Auras melding together

Through the air I creep

I never make a sound

Your aura is almost gone

Time to pounce while you are weak

I start with the transfer to take every last piece

You start to move and thrash

I have to pin you down

Your eyes open but you are not allowed to scream

In the darkness of the night

Lurking above you face to face

Violate the dreams that run a long in your dream

Hold you down and take what I want

All you see is my pale disfigured face

Darkened room with darkened cloak

It is in your face floating above you

I waited too long for the transfer

You broke the bond somehow

You stopped me but I don't know how

Why have you rejected me?

I know you loved me

I screech aloud but only you can hear me

My eyes show you the anger within me

I become withered and pull back

Though you can't move on me

I take enough to get me away from you

I disappear into the darkness

From outside I see the lights turn on

I watch through the window as you shake in terror

In the darkness of the night

Lurking above you face to face

Violate the dreams that run a long in your dream

Hold you down and take what I want

Time to find another one

One just like you

Any easy mind meld

With a loving touch

Enemy of the Righteousness

Think about what I can do

Think about what you can do

Most people ignore

You ignore though

You can if you want to

Nothing is what seems but means everything

The motions in life have consequences

It doesn't matter if it is good or bad

Morality is nothing more than what we have made it

Fiction, False Prophets, and a manmade book

Nothing about it is right

No proof of any facts

Fact check me fuckers

I shall bring you down with me

Let your mind melt with my thoughts

No substance just you and me talking

I can change you and the world

File into the mega churches

You are nothing more than lemmings

Through your money into the basket

They will live rich and you will starve

Hate and anger against people

Oppression against people

From the book that you manipulated to say it

Nothing more than to keep us all in check

Let's have a book burning

Bring the Holy Bible to the fire

Roast a pig and some chicken

Then jump into the hottest point

Nothing is what seems but means everything

The motions in life have consequences

It doesn't matter if it is good or bad

Morality is nothing more than what we have made it

You can't live in a whale, but now a fish

There is no great flood

Science has destroyed your theories

There are no facts in your history

Deceive and destroy the world to your liking

Bring out the wars to send off troops to die

All in the name of your fucking gawd

The time is now

We are here

It's time for reason

If it's better up in the golden gates then go

Unintelligible people are no longer welcome

Take your bigots and the ignorant

Why can't you all just go?

Nothing is what seems but means everything

The motions in life have consequences

It doesn't matter if it is good or bad

Morality is nothing more than what we have made it

Fiction, False Prophets, and a manmade book

There are no facts in your history

It's time for a book burning

Then just fucking leave

Mother May I?

Left in a lonely town

Sidewalks are empty

There are no cars on the road

Its cold outside at three A.M.

Tattooed damaged sign on my chest

Brain dead and terrified

Mother has her boot on my throat

Could you push more to mess me up more?

Left alone to fend for myself

Convert or you're on your own

Mother may I disappoint you again?

You didn't have to keep me

Tattooed damaged sign on my chest

Brain dead and terrified

Mother has her boot on my throat

Could you push more to mess me up more?

Did I make you marry him?

Isn't it a fucking sin when you left?

Nothing but a fucking hypocrite

Now we will end up like you and your mother

Tattooed damaged sign on my chest

Brain dead and terrified

Mother has her boot on my throat

Could you push more to mess me up more?

Leave your children

All for fake shit

189

Push and push us away

You are just like your mother

Tattooed damaged sign on my chest

Brain dead and terrified

Mother has her boot on my throat

Could you push more to mess me up more?

Mother may I ruin your life?

You hold your backseat actions against me

All my life I was looked down at

190

I wasn't a part of your plan

Just an accident

Fucking say it

Tattooed damaged sign on my chest

Brain dead and terrified

Mother has her boot on my throat

Could you push more to mess me up more?

No go away, go away

I will not try anymore

You are on your own now

Next time I see you will be in your pine box

Mothers, Mother, Left a son gone mad

Tattooed damaged sign on my chest

Brain dead and terrified

Mother has her boot on my throat

Could you push more to mess me up more?

Fucking done

No more

192

We are fucking done

I've made my peace

I've made my peace!

You left me alone again

Same shit as before....

Hate Savior, Love Devil

You are my Savior

You are my Devil

You are my love

You are my hate

Blond beauty

Made up in dark makeup

Displaying your art

Always dressed to kill

Tiny little woman

Large in all the right places

You like showing everything off

Perfection at its finest

Oh, those blue eyes

With deadly lips

Perfectly shaped face

However, the neck

Thin and long on its base

You are my Savior

You are my Devil

You are my love

You are my hate

First just marks

The more we grew closer

Marks turned into blood

Finally some violence while we

You place your hands around my neck

I can hardly breathe

My body starts to numb

Lack of oxygen makes me want to black out

Then the greatest feeling in the world happens

Finely tuned machines

Working together

All in motion to satisfy each other

Sexually and emotionally

You are my Savior

197

You are my Devil

You are my love

You are my hate

We are the same

You and I

From the moment we met

Now we are in this moment

Together we conquer everything

We climb to the top past everyone

No one understands are world

We are okay with that

No matter what we are there for each other

To the darkest demonic times

Up to the most angelic moments

Spreading our emotions the only way we know how

You are my Savior

You are my Devil

You are my love

You are my hate

There is no end in sight

As long as we have each other we have everything

My blond beauty

Made up in dark makeup

Displaying your art

Always dressed to kill

Keep singing to me

Lullabies to keep my mind at ease

You are what keeps me stable

Finding you kept me alive

Feels like I cheated death

Blond beauty Savior

Dark eye makeup Devil

Showing your art bringing me love

Dressed to kill to feel the hate

5 Months

It has been five months that I have been trapped inside my home. A spiteful suspension that I somehow became involved in left me alone. All I had was my dog, Maynard, television, and the internet.

At first I thought it would be a quick process for all of this fucked up mess. No, it turned into the longest five months of my life. I stayed home and was paid for it. That's fucked up right? I know it is, but hey I'll take it. In the beginning people that I thought were my friends stayed by my side. Then most people started to slip away from my life.

People that I considered close friends were no longer even trying to communicate. There was a handful that kept in touch and keeping me in the loop. My world kept growing smaller and smaller. My mother dropped her children before the holidays. She had become this Jesus fucking freak. She believed my sister drank too much and said she should stop and join Jesus. My dear brother through his fucked up life is gay and well that's just not allowed in her eyes. I never had the straight on talk. She doesn't have the balls to challenge me because I am too smart for her and know almost every counter point. However being a tattooed freak and an Atheist doesn't help even though Jesus never turned anyone away, makes you think. All that meant was that I was on my own with one friend in it that I hardly see and the others that did still talk to me was over half an hour away or more.

In the beginning I began watching every movie I could get on Netflix. I binged on television shows and watched movie after movie from the time I woke until the time I went to bed. There is now a permanent ass mark on my couch. What do you do when you run out of movies though? I know it seems hard since Netflix has a grand amount of movies and shows, but I ran out. Then the boredom came and that's when I started to write more. The pages before this are more than just poems, thoughts or songs. They are of greater learning. What I learned though was very valuable, to me. I finally understood what it was like to be by myself. I finally learned who I was and who I wanted to meet and to be with. I figured that out with movies and television. However, I took it as impossible because what happens in movies never happens in real life. All it took was a five to ten minute conversation with someone to figure out there are people that are like me. I want to thank that person but may never be able to unless she reads this book, then I say thank you.

What I figured out with all of that was I am in a home that is mine and I can do whatever the fuck I want and no one is going to tell me no. This is my house to remodel and to fix up. A year and a half and I just never did anything with it. Then I started. I did a lot of work to personalize things to my liking. Imagine my liking. I don't have to worry about anything, it was liberating. I am free. It doesn't matter what happens. I am still going to be here. I will have Maynard to keep me company and I am okay with that. For this I just want to say that the fucked up, stupid, idiotic way I was put on administrative leave, I feel no ill will towards that person. It has turned out to be an experience that I needed to have. However, I go back in a week, and I am terrified. The stress that left me is coming back and I don't like it. I have to stay myself. Continue being me. Being the Straight Edge, artistic, liberal, persona that I have become, atoolcircle....

ATOOLCIRCLE

Round I go in the circle

Again and again

Just another cog

The perfect tool

Living and repeating lives

All in just one life

Same damn thing in different times

Repeating my life over and over

Again and again

Round I go in the circle

The perfect tool

Just another cog

Needy and helpless

Finding a reason to get close

Entering the crack that is in your mind

What is it that you need?

Just another cog

Round I go in the circle

The perfect tool

Again and again

With you I give you what you need

I manipulate you into staying

Then it gets thrown back at me

All when the work has been done

The perfect tool

Just another cog

Again and again

Round I go in the circle

A man that lays and waits

Time passes by

The new circuit

The grander echo into my life

Round I go in the circle

Again and again

Just another cog

The perfect tool

Always living my Ouroboros

Over and over

Living the same life

Each is different but the principal is the same

Again and again

The perfect tool

Just another cog

Round I go in the circle

Here we are now again

Just like before

There is nothing new

Except the body

The concept stays the same

I have found myself in an infinite loop

Each one is different in their own ways

I help you and show you a better future

Rewarded with sexual favors

Like there is no soul only a body

Just another cog

Round I go in the circle

Again and again

The perfect tool

Only an outer shell to reverse the manipulation

Use your body to get what you want from me

I stand naked and blind in front of you filled with emotion

All just to have the tower of trust burned down

Keep your mind straight

All you have to be is sober

Just take my hand

I need to know if you feel

Have you ever felt

Left out to hang

Stripped down with a broken mind

Left out to hang

Stripped down with a broken body

The perfect tool for the job

Another cog in your wheel of life

Round I go in circles that are just the same person but different bodies

Again and again and again and again

The calculations of me getting my turn should have happened

However, I may never get my turn

All I see is the same old thing and the same old song

Here I am, ready to be abused

All there has to be is a charge

The electrical flow

Desperate to find my doppelganger

I am tired of being everyone's abused tool

Spit out and stomped upon as waste

Round I go in the circle

Again and again

Just another cog

The perfect tool

A tool for someone's expense

A tool circle

A tool for someone's pleasure

In life a repeated circle

Only to be used as a tool

A piece of life that is executed repeatedly never
stopping....

I am atoolcircle

Doppelganger World

Tic Toc Tic Toc

Shit Fuck Shit Fuck

Time is a placement used for events

The event of life has been wasted

Waiting too fucking long

To fucking long

There she was so close

Here I could reach and touch

Sight seen and glances taken

Everything seemed to make sense

Time is a placement used for events

The event of life has been wasted

Waiting too fucking long

Now the event has passed

Where was my head

It has been a long time

I forgot how to make events happen

Scared I thought the dream would just combine into one

Time is a placement used for events

The event of life has been wasted

Waiting too fucking long

Now the event has fucking passed

Hopes of atomic mind melding

Seeing things in each other's dreams

Two singular beings

Turning into one world unit

Time is a placement used for events

The event of life has been wasted

Waiting too fucking long

Now the event has been pissed away

Never knew that there was another world with any life

Thought this was the only planet that sustained intelligent life

Then the tether caught on another world

Never thought there would be a doppelganger to my world

Mirrored in seemingly everyway

That is the key to all of space

Though the key never seemed to ever be turned

The dream of our worlds combining slipped away

Time is a placement used for events

The event of life has been wasted

Waiting too fucking long

Now the event has passed by like there was no choice

This world will wait for the next event

Nothing lasts forever

Everyone makes their own choices

The key will eventually turn

For now the tether will be small between our worlds

Tether our worlds

We swing around each other like the universe and the sun

Either the sun will die or the worlds will collide

Time is a placement used for events

The event of life has been wasted

Waiting too fucking long

Now the event has passed and things seemed fucked

The world feels like it's on fire

Singularity of the world

Wasting the dream

It's Just an Empty Home

Open the door to the cold dark house

I walk in and things are just there

There is no one inside

No one to lust or love for

Just an empty home

Spent time fixing myself and looking back at those events

Reached deep inside and found a new part of myself

I learned how to put the puzzle pieces together

Then it all seemed to make sense

It's just an empty home

I walk in and things are just there

No one to lust after

There's no one to love here

Time has passed on

I go to familiar places and get smacked down

Not by the people but by myself

These are not my people

They are not like me

Lies and lies

It seems like junior high here

Talk and rumors

At the end of the day I am glad to be away

Though I tremble to go home

It's just an empty home

I walk in and things are just there

No one to lust after

There's no one to love here

There's no one to love out there

There's only manipulation

There's no intelligible connection with anyone

There's not even someone to lust over

No love, no lust, no sex, no fucking

Empty home is always a cold home

Possessions are just items

However I wouldn't mind being a possession

It's just an empty home

I walk in and things are just there

No one to lust after

There's no one to love here

I know that I messed up my life

I know that I have hurt people that have loved me

I know that I have destroyed families

I know that I deserve what I am getting

It's ok

Don't feel for me

Leave me be

The darkness and the cold will be my comfort.

It's just an empty home

I walk in and things are just there

No one to lust after

There's no one to love here

Empty home

Just obsessional items

No one wants to lust after me

There is no one left who will love someone like me

226

Someone like me

Someone like me

No one is like me

No one is like me

No one wants crazy

You don't want fucking crazy me

It's just an empty fucking home

I walk in and obsessions and possessions

No one waiting who wants to just fuck

There's no one to love me in here out there

I am just by myself

Forever Intertwined

While you sleep

Come find me standing over you

I will be waiting for you here

By your bed while your asleep

Another night a long time ago

You stood by my side while I slept

I came to find you but I was lost

Then I seen you leave when I found my way there

Once upon a time we met in dream land

We shared stories and talked for eternity

The others never bothered us

They just walked around talking to each other

Together we stayed until the sun rose

Then one night you came over

You were early I wasn't a sleep yet

Though I heard you moving around

I waited but feel asleep for you to come through my
bedroom door

While you sleep

Come find me standing over you

I will be waiting for you here

229

By your bed while your asleep

Another night a long time ago

You stood by my side while I slept

I came to find you but I was lost

Then I seen you leave when I found my way there

We found out together we can do anything

All we need is our minds, hearts and souls

Together in unison we control our worlds

All we have to do is walk through the door

When we do no matter what

I know you will be there

If to just pick me up again

Just like if you were down I'd pull you back

Though we know when

Each one of us can tell

When one is down

We will meet up and see each other

While you sleep

Come find me standing over you

I will be waiting for you here

By your bed while your asleep

Another night a long time ago

You stood by my side while I slept

I came to find you but I was lost

Then I seen you leave when I found my way there

Sometimes I wish we could wake up

Sit up in bed and look at each other

Then lie back down and pull each other close

Using our physical selves to communicate

Though I know certain things will never happen

You also know that things will never happen

We will always be able to see each other

Mad and cold we will travel massive millage

Just to connect

Though both of us will always know

Knowledge of our souls connecting

With our hearts growing closer

We are forever intertwined

While you sleep

Come find me standing over you

I will be waiting for you here

By your bed while your asleep

Another night a long time ago

You stood by my side while I slept

I came to find you but I was lost

Then I seen you leave when I found my way there

Not touching skin to skin

Not exploring each other

Not seeing face to face

Not ever really knowing is killing both of us.

It's the choices we have made

Maybe in the next plain or life

This is just the way it is

Continue with our adventures

I never want to lose you and me

Life is an Imagination of Ourselves

Imagine all of our worlds bouncing off each other like balls hitting each other. The main objective is to control your world. You cannot stop another's world. Everyone has a choice on everything we do which will ripple through the energies of our own personal world. Peace, love, and harmony in one's self are the greatest gift to your being. Take control of your worlds, be kind to others worlds, and intern the other worlds should be kind to you. It is not doing unto others because we are only based upon positive and negative energies. There is no true reality only what we encompass ourselves with, hence our own personal worlds. We all have full control and are fully aware of our own consciousness and the realities around us. It is up to the world to choose and to recognize which force of energy they choose to embrace.

Kindness between worlds is key for the energy field. When one world interacts with another it should embrace it as if it brings your world what it seeks. It does not matter what type of energy you are as long as it is what the world seeks. If one world seeks out negative energy and brings negative energies into their world then that is what that world wants. Not all worlds realize their effect of the energies around them and are really never in control and go with the matter flow. Then there are the positive worlds that attract other positive worlds to their world. For the most part those worlds seem happier and interact positively with each other. Next we have the negative world that have full composition of their world and know they are negative but to them there is no difference in the negative or positive there is only energy to be used from others in the matter field. They embrace only action equal to another action. Lastly we have the positive world that is more than just a positive to one world to another. These worlds meld in mind and infinite matter since there is no time. They are connected to each other by energies constantly moving to one another. These worlds help, listen, give, to each other and cannot be separated. They continue to learn and delve deeper into the energy pool and try to find more and learn more about the matter that is around them. The world wants only to reach a level of not belief but knowing and understanding. These worlds also have full knowledge of the other worlds and what type of energy that surrounds the other worlds. Both superior worlds that connect with their own kind, like trying to meet

237

a doppelganger like world to be connected to. My world is to help, listen, give, and learn, while doing a cannon ball into the energy pool to learn more.

Liberal Socialist

Mary, Mary, Mary

Why did you lie?

How come you let the lie live?

Why not just abort?

Mary, Mary, Mary

Why did you help cheat this world?

How can you look at us now?

Why would you allow the injustices?

Mary, Mary, Mary

Why did you bring war?

How did you let children die?

Why do you let things happen in his name?

Mary, Mary, Mary

You could have kept the peace

Never going to that manger

Should have stayed away from that inn

Mary, Mary, Mary

Don't shine that light

Making the star bright

For three fouls to follow

Mary, Mary, Mary

The indoctrination of the masses started that night

For over two thousand years now

People follow a false Prophet

Mary, Mary, Mary

The Bible has been manipulated to indoctrinate

Pointing us in the moral compass that people in charge want us to be

Realistically Jesus was just a Liberal Socialist.

Mary, Mary, Mary

What do you think of that?

A Socialist that wanted to help the poor!

Not to leave them under an overpass to starve.

All he was is some guy that was a Liberal.

Multi-Personality Bi-Polar Die-Bye

I'm back. Six months and I am still the best in the world. Here I am you couldn't take me fucking down. I stand here not to just rub it in. I am here to change it all and fuck with all of you. It's funny how ninety percent of you forgot about me or talked shit and here I am showing your ass up. Here is a fucking razor blade go take yourself.

I don't mean what I say. I have a new attitude. I love everyone and want know harm to anyone. Let's kick back and laugh all night telling a joke or two. Yes high, how are you? Shake my hand, give me a hug, do you have a baby for me to kiss? I feel like I am running for office. I am so glad to see you, how was your vacation? You look good.

Over six months of waiting for the phone to ring. Just an answer and nothing ever came for days to weeks. Fucking sixty pounds lost to stress, that's my fucking diet quit asking what did it. Some said pray to God and he will answer your prayers. Fuck that there isn't one. No one fucks people like this and the things that I seen on the television. There isn't faith in this house.

It's ok I have my family and my friends. We talk and love one another we will be all fine with each other. A group text with others in my situation to keep us up together so our mood doesn't fall to a new low, the vacation was a great time. Netflix loved me, made their money off of me. Finish this book and now I push it all out to you so you all know what I thought of, the time before and past.

Listen to the voices they all say something different. Each thought different, pushing and pushing fucking with

244

me. I make mistakes and take things to new levels in my mind and I get kicked when I am already down. Then I call my mommy, sorry I am a fucking an adult and I know that Jesus isn't real because my head isn't stuck up my ass. I know let's just not talk anymore, it's not like you had your foot cut off. Fuck it, yeah I said fuck what does it matter anymore. Pissed at me here is a knife take care of that problem.

Phone me to see if I am ok, see if I am still alive. I appreciate the fact that you care. It means a lot to me right now. I am so scared but there is patience from you and some of the others. Though the calls become less and less, lose them in time, and I mess up and I turn special people away from me. I moved here to get away and now I am gone. I have a few constants. Then it almost comes down to one and it meant everything that it was the fact that it was you. I fucked up and I was lost without the others.

Ahhh... The Bi-polar fuck you says fuck me to those who pushed me down and stomped on me. You forgot about me and pushed me away and didn't bother to call or visit. What am I? Who am I? What the fuck I do to the entire world for you to disappear out of my fucking life. When is it my fucking turn? Shitty fucking life since the start, I know I was the mistake, ruined lives, not my fucking problem. Dealt with what's always been in front of me. Most of you would have taken the gun and followed Kurt or maybe been killed. Since 01' it's been the same for me in my modern life.

I am so glad that most of you have missed me. I am glad that most of you wanted me back. You all show you that you care, I love you to. I am glad to be back to do my duty for my wonderful country and do something great for the world. Keeping you safe and your family, I need no thank you it's ok I know that you appreciate me when you yell in my face and tell me to fuck off.

I know it's hard for you to fucking understand. This is me now no more bi-polar shit. Don't give a shit what you think of me anymore. I know who I am now. No more bitches that use and abuse me. Yeah do things for you and reward with sexual fucking favors but you really don't fucking like it! Then why am I here if you don't mean it! Fuck that I am gone. Over and over and over, you get the fucking point.

Want to know what I did on my fucking vacation? I realized there is mean people out there. There are bitches that will blow you for what they want. I know that most of the people that are my friends are not. I am a used abused beat up three legged dog. Don't feel bad, fuck you. I am rebuilding, I know what has happened in my life and I am alone moving forward. The hand full that is beside me I love you and don't ever want to lose you, again.

Fuckers I am BACK! I am Back! I know what I want and I am going to take it. I don't need you if you are not in my life now. I don't need a new member of my own made family, fuck blood, I'll take water, and I've been on my own for way to long. Step by step I'll take what I want and take prisoners if I want. I will continue to climb this mountain and I will continue to do it without most of you and I am ok with that. Those who know can suck a dick and fuck themselves.

I know this all seems mean and maybe too real. Sometimes you just have to scream and yell and put everything in place. This is the perspective. This is the real way. Don't look at me differently now. Everyone has this inside of them; it's just finally had to come out of me, because I am ok with myself now. That's the important thing. I know who I am now. It's taken all these years and I know who I am and what I want. I am still the same loving giving person that I have always been, but even more. I am just not going to be fooled like I was before. The hand full of people from work, my boys, the very little amount of blood, and others it's still me, don't be scared, I love you all. However, to everyone else...

The Best in the World is back and taking what is his.

I'm sorry to those I scared, really it's still the abnormal me.

Should I have written this?

Demon

Here we are

Let's kick out of the conscious

Find the little angel that sits on my shoulder

Squash the bitch

Time to find that little demon on the other side of me

Can you hear me?

I am here to whisper in your ear

I'll be the one that tells you right from wrong

What is real and just a dream

Don't sit around and wait

You need to act fast

This is my attack

Can you feel the hate?

Can you hear me?

I am here to whisper in your ear

I'll be the one that tells right from wrong

What is real and just a dream, but it's all wrong

I know I said shit in the past

Things that I cannot be forgiven for

I don't want to be forgiven or forgotten

That was just a yesterday, if yesterday was a few years
ago

Can you hear me?

I am here to whisper in your ear

I'll be the one that tells right from wrong

What is real and just a dream

Should have killed the angel a long time ago

Feeling free with myself

I know that I have found myself

Still need to act out from the past to make up for lost time

I learned a lot from my little demon

Sitting on my shoulder

Shouting in my ear

Ignored before but now I see I should have listened to
every syllable

Can you hear me?

I am here to whisper in your ear

I'll be the one that tells right from wrong

What's real and just a dream, it was all a nightmare

The life from the beginning

The life until now

Nightmare to wonderland

No more time to fear and steer clear

Time to play and unleash the demon

Can you hear me?

I am here to whisper in your ear

I'll be the one that tells right from wrong

What is real?

What is not?

Demon killed the angel of conscious

Now I am free be me

Wasteland

What is real and what is not?

Dreams are reality

Reality is a dream

Everything is a blur without lines

We seem to have put lines on everything

Ownership on everything

Yet no one can really own anything

Nothing is really here

Nature and evolution have made us the way we are

Indoctrinated into the idea of possession

Pushed into beliefs

A way of life created by a man made God

If God is man then we all are God's

We can then do whatever we want

We placed value on metals turned to coin

We placed value on paper made into money

We placed value on things that can be traded

If we took all of it and burned it all

Nothing would change

Society would still stand

It would take some time

We would evolve back into a primitive time

I want that time

The time of sharing

Peace and good will

No more hate and anger

Only love for one another

If only we could except these things

Then only could the world move forward

Yet we stay here and kill

Practice pollution

Slowly killing the thing that keeps alive

The thing that we all say we love but don't care about
after we are gone

Though if God is manmade and you could reenergize and
be reborn

Then you should care

If not for that

Then for the love of all other creatures to come

We take advantage, use, abuse, waste, hate, love, and destroy

Everything on everyone and everything

If life were a dream then it wouldn't matter

Though its not and we should be considerate towards others and things

Just so we can evolve into intelligible creature that is orgasmic

Trusted Razor Blood

There is finally someone here with me

All this time you were right in front of me

Always honest and caring, building a foundation

The foundation of a trusted bond

With trust we found faith in each other

Together we loved

We spent all our time together

Inseparable with the hands of time standing still

Our hearts would speed up fast and glow through our
skin

My heart and your heart

Two muscles moving as one

I took you into my head

You took all of me into you

Connected and bonded by love, trust, and now our souls

We kept each other's evil and darkness within each other

I hid your evil in my soul

You hid my darkness inside your loving world

Two flesh beings becoming one

No one else understood you

I scared everyone with my dimness

You took it in stride with you

No outer parts stopped us from being one

United inside each other

Loving

Caressing

Trusting

Faith

Needing

Feeding

Until the moon moved the stars

With Venus imploding into Mars

Our universe began to quake

Irrational behavior

Normal relationship things

No, no it was more

My darkness began to scare you

I enjoyed your false evilness that was never real

With fakeness and lies

Our separation became brutal

The hate that was reserved and loved inside came pouring
out

We couldn't help each other

The things we loved bothered us

The trust slipped away

Our hearts broke apart

Soul lines clipped and taken back

No more love

Time apart

Bringing thoughts together in the dark places

I still loved you

We will be together again

Soaked in tears and blood

Rusted Razor Blood

Clamped hand around the handle

Dripping from the mess

Heart racing with your mind trying to catch up

Why did it have to come to this?

My boots move the floor boards as I grow close

Knife in my hand I look down at you as you sleep

My mind commands me to do this to you

It tells me that you deserve to suffer

Push and abuse

A man can only take so much

Used and fooled

A man can only take so much

That's what they say

The voice plunges the knife

Deep down into your chest

Into the rib cage

Right the cold black heart

How could you not hear me?

You must have wanted to die

This is what you wanted

Push me to put you down

Lay in your own pool of blood

It tastes fucking great

My body drips from your blood

While I repeatedly stab you

Walked into the bathroom

Looked in the mirror

Found myself a mess

The soul in these eyes are gone

Murderer, Murderer

Stabbing you, Stabbing you

Pushed to hate by lies

The voices say it's okay.

Murderer, Murderer

Stabbing you, Stabbed you

Pushed to hate by lies

The voices say it's okay.

Now you mean nothing

My friends tell me it was well worth it

It's just them and me now

Enjoy the hole I made for you

Do you like it?

Is it deep enough?

Are you going to be cold?

You no longer control me

Why do I still hear you in my head?

How are you speaking?

You're fucking dead in the backyard

Leave me alone!

Leave me alone!

Leave me

Fine okay you want me?

I'll come be with you

I give myself to you

Rusted razor blade in hand

Slice the wrist, slice the other wrist

Don't worry I am coming

I see me in the bathroom on the floor

There is a mass amount of blood

The tile is turned red

There you are holding me after finding me

I didn't mean to make you cry

I didn't want to make you hurt like this

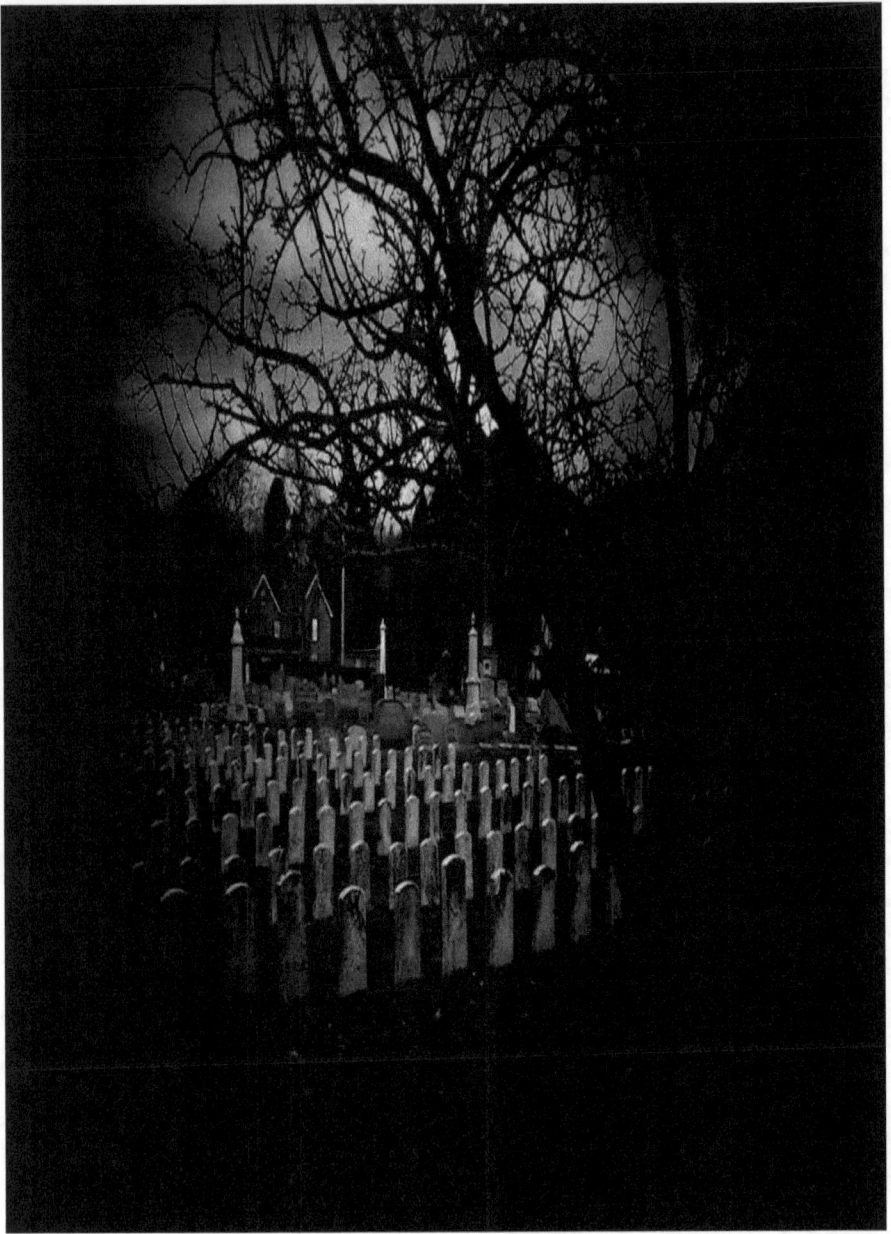

How to Follow Me:

http://atoolcircle666.wix.com/atoolcircle#!home/mainPage/mainPage/imagejy1

https://twitter.com/atoolcircle

https://plus.google.com/u/0/+JustinSettleatoolcircle/posts

https://www.facebook.com/groups/134231190056739/

http://instagram.com/atoolcircle

https://www.youtube.com/user/atoolcircle666